Funky Winkerbean

by TOM BATIUK

For Cathy

by TOM BATIUK

NANTIER ○ BEALL ○ MINOUSTCHINE

Publishing inc.

new york

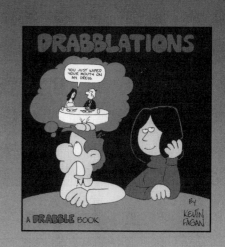

ISBN 1-56163-266-X
©1995, 1996, 1998, 2000 Batom, Inc.
Distributed by North America
Syndicate, Inc. All Rights Reserved.
Printed in Canada

5   4   3   2   1

SO I FIGURED BY HAVING SUSAN SUBMIT SOME OF HER POEMS TO THE SCHOOL NEWSPAPER, IT WOULD HELP DRAW HER OUT AND GET HER MORE INVOLVED IN SCHOOL ACTIVITIES!

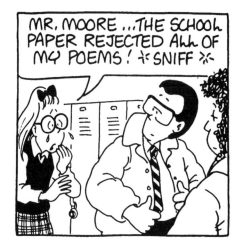

MR. MOORE...THE SCHOOL PAPER REJECTED ALL OF MY POEMS! ☀SNIFF☀

WELL, THERE GOES MY 'TEACHER OF THE YEAR' AWARD...

YOU KNOW...I THINK I'LL GO GET AN EARLY JUMP ON BUS DUTY...

I KNOW IT'S DISAPPOINTING TO HAVE YOUR POEMS TURNED DOWN BY THE SCHOOL PAPER, SUSAN...

BUT I THOUGHT THOMAS GRAY'S 'ELEGY WRITTEN IN A COUNTRY CHURCHYARD' MIGHT HELP YOU PUT IT IN PERSPECTIVE!

'FULL MANY A GEM OF PUREST RAY SERENE THE DARK UNFATHOMED CAVES OF OCEAN BEAR: FULL MANY A FLOWER IS BORN TO BLUSH UNSEEN, AND WASTE ITS SWEETNESS ON THE DESERT AIR.'

SUSAN IS A BRIGHT STUDENT, BUT SHE LACKS CONFIDENCE IN HERSELF!

I THOUGHT MAYBE IF I COULD ENCOURAGE HER WRITING ABILITY, I COULD BOOST HER SELF-ESTEEM A LITTLE.

FUNKY WINKERBEAN by TOM BATIUK

HERE'S MR. MOORE AT HIS SENIOR PROM!

Senior Prom

THAT'S ODD...

I WONDER WHY MR. MOORE'S PROM DATE ISN'T PICTURED WITH HIM?

FACE IT, LES ... THE PROM'S JUST ABOUT OVER... MELISSA ISN'T COMING BACK FROM THE RESTROOM!

WELL, I'LL SHOW HER! IF SHE ISN'T BACK IN TWO MINUTES ... I'M DRINKING THIS OTHER PUNCH!

✶SIGH✶ SHE WAS PROBABLY THE QUEEN OF THE PROM AND WAS OFF PERFORMING SOME OFFICIAL FUNCTION!

I CAN'T BELIEVE THEY KEEP THE YEARBOOK FROM MR. MOORE'S GRADUATING CLASS OUT IN THE OPEN LIKE THIS!

I WOULD'VE THOUGHT IT WOULD BE KEPT UNDER GLASS IN A SPECIAL CASE!

MR. MOORE... WHY WASN'T YOUR DATE SHOWN IN THIS PROM PICTURE FROM YOUR SENIOR YEARBOOK?

BECAUSE SHE EXCUSED HERSELF TO GO TO THE RESTROOM WHEN WE GOT TO THE PROM AND I NEVER SAW HER THE REST OF THE NIGHT!

WHAT A KIDDER! I LOVE HIS SENSE OF HUMOR!

I'VE RUN OFF TEST COPIES FOR TOMORROW, GRADED ALL OF YOUR PAPERS AND ENTERED THE GRADES IN YOUR GRADEBOOK! IS THERE ANYTHING ELSE THAT I CAN DO?

THANKS, BUT I DON'T THINK SO, SUSAN... UNLESS YOU'D LIKE TO GO OUT AND WAX MY CAR.

NO PROBLEM!

NO, WAIT, THAT WAS A JOKE!

SO I MENTIONED THAT I WANTED TO GET A LITTLE EXERCISE AND BULL INVITED ME TO STOP BY TO PLAY SOME BASKETBALL AT THE 'Y' WEDNESDAY NIGHT!

NO KIDDING... YOU'RE GOING TO PLAY IN THE WEDNESDAY NIGHT Y-BALL LEAGUE!?

DO YOU WANT ME TO CALL 911 NOW AND HAVE THEM ON STANDBY?

WHAT'S WRONG WITH THE WEDNESDAY NIGHT Y-BALL LEAGUE?

NOTHING... IT'S JUST THAT THEY HAVE A REPUTATION FOR BEING A TAD VIOLENT!

VIOLENT!?

I HEARD THAT INSTEAD OF DRINKING GATORADE... THEY JUST CHUG PURE TESTOSTERONE!

SO LES IS PLAYING BASKETBALL A THE 'Y' TONIGHT?

YEP! I WONDER HOW HE'S DOING!

THIS SOCK SHOULD STOP THE BLEEDING!

HERE ARE HIS GLASSES!

AND HERE ARE THE REST OF HIS GLASSES!

FUNKY WINKERBEAN

BY TOM BATIUK

WE WANT TO KNOW WHY YOU MARKED ALL OF OUR ANSWERS WRONG!

BECAUSE THEY WEREN'T RIGHT!

IF YOU HAD TAKEN THE TIME TO READ CHAPTER TWENTY LIKE YOU WERE SUPPOSED TO...

YOU WOULD'VE FOUND ALL THE ANSWERS FOR YOUR WORKSHEET QUESTIONS!

BUT YOU DIDN'T SAY WE HAD TO <u>READ</u> CHAPTER TWENTY... YOU JUST SAID WE HAD TO GO THROUGH IT!

SHE'S RIGHT! YOU SPECIFICALLY SAID: 'TO FIND THE ANSWERS, <u>GO THROUGH</u> CHAPTER TWENTY!'

SUSAN AND I HAVE BEEN TALKING ABOUT HAVING OUR POETRY CLUB PUT OUT A SCHOOL LITERARY MAGAZINE, SADIE!

I DIDN'T KNOW PEOPLE COULD DO THAT!

WHERE DO YOU THINK MAGAZINES COME FROM?

THE SUPERMARKET!

IF OUR POETRY CLUB IS GOING TO PUT OUT A LITERARY MAGAZINE, WE'LL NEED TO DECIDE HOW OFTEN WE'RE GOING TO MEET TO WORK ON IT!

EVERY NIGHT!

DON'T YOU THINK EVERY NIGHT IS A BIT MUCH?

OKAY... WE'LL SKIP SATURDAYS AND SUNDAYS!

HAVE YOU TWO COME UP WITH ANY TITLES FOR THE LITERARY MAGAZINE?

HOW ABOUT 'ELYSIAN FIELDS'?

NOT BAD, SUSAN... WHAT HAVE YOU GOT, SADIE?

'THE WESTVIEW HIGH SCHOOL LITERARY MAGAZINE'!

WELL, WHAT IT LACKS IN ROMANCE... IT CERTAINLY MAKES UP FOR IN DIRECTNESS...

Funky Winkerbean

BY TOM BATIUK

METER
STANZA
VERSE

WELL, MR. MOORE...?

WHAT DO YOU THINK?

I THINK THIS POEM YOU WROTE IS VERY GOOD, SUSAN ... BUT IT COULD BE BETTER!

STA
VE

IT'S ALMOST AS IF YOU'RE PUTTING TOO MUCH PRESSURE ON YOURSELF AND FORCING THINGS TOO MUCH!

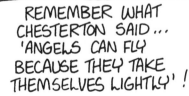

REMEMBER WHAT CHESTERTON SAID... 'ANGELS CAN FLY BECAUSE THEY TAKE THEMSELVES LIGHTLY'!

METE
STAN
VE

HE THINKS I'M AN ANGEL!

...Careful not to break the tender wings, Of this new love I've found.

OKAY, SUSAN ... I'VE READ YOUR POEM...

YOU CAN OPEN YOUR EYES NOW!

YOUR POEM PROVIDES A REAL INSIGHT INTO THE HUMAN CONDITION, SUSAN...

WHICH IS WHAT EVERY WORK OF ART STRIVES TO DO... I THINK IT'S PERFECT FOR THE LITERARY MAGAZINE!

DO YOU NEED ANY HELP WITH THE LITERARY MAGAZINE, SUSAN?

SURE, SADIE ... YOU COULD HELP ME PROOF AND PASTE UP THESE LAYOUTS!

DID I FORGET TO MENTION THAT WAS A TOKEN OFFER?

18

SO IF AN EDITOR WAS INTERESTED IN ONE OF YOUR STORIES, BUT HE WANTED YOU TO MAKE SOME CHANGES... YOU'D JUST GO AHEAD AND MAKE THEM?

UH-HUH... ONE THING YOU LEARN VERY QUICKLY AS A WRITER...

IS TO NEVER ARGUE WITH SOMEONE WHO BUYS INK BY THE BARREL!

THAT CLIQUE THAT SADIE SUMMERS RUNS WITH IS PRETTY FORMIDABLE, ISN'T IT?

I'LL SAY!

IT'S THE FIRST ONE IN THE HISTORY OF THE SCHOOL TO ACTUALLY BE INCORPORATED!

I HAVEN'T SEEN THE COACH THIS MORNING!

YEAH... I KNOW! HE TOOK HIS SENIORS ON A FIELD TRIP!

OH YEAH... WHERE TO? THE CINEMA SEVEN AT THE MALL?

I'M TELLING HIM YOU SAID THAT!

YOU ALWAYS DID SEEM LIKE A SNITCH!

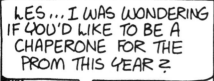

I'VE BEEN SITTING HERE WITH THIS AIRPLANE TICKET TO SEATTLE THAT LISA SENT ME...

AND I'VE BEEN TRYING TO FIGURE OUT WHAT IT ALL MEANS...

HELLO... ANYBODY HOME?

KNOCK KNOCK

YOU CERTAINLY LOOK MORE RELAXED THAN YESTERDAY!

I AM!

I'VE DECIDED THAT I'M GOING TO TAKE THOSE AIRPLANE TICKETS THAT LISA SENT ME AND GO VISIT HER IN SEATTLE OVER SPRING BREAK...

AND WHILE I'M THERE I'M GOING TO POP THE QUESTION!

CHOKE! GASP!

NOW YOU DON'T LOOK SO GOOD!

SO ARE YOU GOING ANYWHERE FOR YOUR SPRING BREAK, MR. MOORE?

YEAH, AS A MATTER OF FACT I'M GOING TO SEATTLE!

POOR GUY... HE HASN'T GOT A CLUE!

23

CALL IT THE INTUITION THAT I INHERITED FROM MY GRANDMOTHER, FUNKY...

BUT I HAVE A FEELING THAT LES IS POPPING THE QUESTION TO LISA AT THIS VERY MOMENT!

WELL?

SURE... I'LL GO TO THE PROM WITH YOU, LES!

HOW WAS LISA AND SEATTLE?

GREAT!

SO DID YOU POP THE QUESTION?

YEP...

AND SHE SAID 'YES'!

GULP!

SO YOU ACTUALLY POPPED THE QUESTION TO LISA AND SHE SAID 'YES'?

THAT'S RIGHT... OF COURSE, IT DEPENDS ON WHETHER OR NOT SHE CAN GET A COUPLE OF DAYS OFF...

BUT, IF SHE CAN, SHE FIGURED 'WHAT THE HECK... WHY NOT?'!

LET ME SEE IF I UNDERSTAND THIS...

YOU POPPED THE QUESTION TO LISA AND SHE RESPONDED BY SAYING, 'WHAT THE HECK... WHY NOT?'!?

SURE! IT'S NOT REALLY THAT BIG A DEAL...

IT'S JUST SOMETHING WE THOUGHT WOULD BE FUN TO DO AS A LARK!

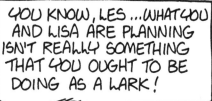

YOU KNOW, LES... WHAT YOU AND LISA ARE PLANNING ISN'T REALLY SOMETHING THAT YOU OUGHT TO BE DOING AS A LARK!

I MEAN, FOR ONE THING, THERE ARE THE FINANCIAL ASPECTS TO CONSIDER!

WELL, I'LL CHECK IT OUT!

AND IF IT'S GOING TO COST TOO MUCH... WE WON'T DO IT!

FUNKY JUST TOLD ME THE GOOD NEWS, LES, AND I WANTED YOU TO KNOW YOU COULD HAVE YOUR RECEPTION HERE AT MONTONI'S ... ON THE HOUSE!

UH, GEE... THAT'S REALLY NICE, TONY ... BUT I JUST FIGURED THAT WE'D BE GOING OUT TO EAT BY OURSELVES AFTER THE PROM!

I'LL STRANGLE HIM ... NO, THAT'S TOO QUICK ...

WE'VE GOT A STAFF MEETING THURSDAY!?

YEAH... IT'S TO ANSWER QUESTIONS ABOUT THE NEW OUTCOME-BASED EDUCATION PLAN!

SO WHAT DO YOU MAKE OF THIS NEW PROGRAM THAT THE ADMINISTRATION IS PUSHING, LINDA?

I REALLY DON'T HAVE ANY PROBLEM WITH THE IDEA OF OUTCOME-BASED EDUCATION, LES...

BUT IF THEY REALLY WANT TO IMPROVE THE QUALITY OF EDUCATION HERE AT WESTVIEW...

THEY'D BE BETTER OFF CONCENTRATING ON INCOME-BASED EDUCATORS!

AND SO BASICALLY, LISA... THIS SCHOOL YEAR IS GOING MUCH BETTER FOR ME THAN LAST YEAR... IN FACT, MY POETRY CLUB JUST PUBLISHED THE SCHOOL'S FIRST LITERARY MAGAZINE!

I FINALLY FEEL LIKE I BELONG, AND CAN JUST RELAX AND ENJOY BEING A TEACHER!

WALTER... HAVE YOU SEEN THIS FILTH THAT BECKY BROUGHT HOME FROM SCHOOL?

WESTVIEW LITERARY MAGAZINE

THIS IS FROM THE PRINCIPAL!

OH, OH... IT LOOKS LIKE ONE OF YOU SCHOLARS HAS TO GO TO THE OFFICE!

OH, IT'S FOR ME...

LES, WE'VE HAD A COMPLAINT ABOUT THE LITERARY MAGAZINE THAT YOUR POETRY CLUB HAS PUT OUT!

PRINCIPAL

OH, OH... WAS THERE A GRAMMATICAL ERROR OR SOMETHING?

WE SHOULD BE SO LUCKY!

SHOULD I BE SITTING DOWN OR JUST LYING ON THE FLOOR?

LES... BECKY BLACKBURN'S MOTHER THINKS THAT YOUR POETRY CLUB'S LITERARY MAGAZINE SHOULD BE BANNED AND THAT YOU SHOULD BE FIRED!

OH...

WHAT DID SHE THINK ABOUT THE COLORS WE CHOSE FOR THE COVER?

EXACTLY WHAT IS IT ABOUT THE LITERARY MAGAZINE THAT MRS. BLACKBURN DOESN'T LIKE?

HERE'S A FLIER SHE'S HANDING OUT WITH THE PART SHE FINDS OBJECTIONABLE!

ONE WORD!? ISN'T THAT TAKING THINGS A BIT OUT OF CONTEXT!?

SO HOW ARE YOU GOING TO RESPOND TO MRS. BLACKBURN'S COMPLAINT ABOUT OUR LITERARY MAGAZINE, FRED?

I HAVEN'T DECIDED... AND UNTIL I DO, I WANT TO KEEP A LID ON THIS THING BEFORE TOO MANY PEOPLE GET WIND OF IT!

GOOD NEWS, MR. MOORE! OUR LITERARY MAGAZINE IS A COMPLETE SELLOUT!

WHAT'S THAT YOU'RE HIDING BETWEEN THE MATTRESSES, MIKE?

IT'S JUST A COPY OF PENTHOUSE, DAD!

GOOD! FOR A SECOND THERE I THOUGHT IT WAS A COPY OF THE WESTVIEW LITERARY MAGAZINE!

MMPH! MMPH!

FRED... THE PANEL OF FACULTY AND STUDENTS THAT YOU PUT TOGETHER IS DEADLOCKED ON WHETHER OR NOT THIS WESTVIEW LITERARY MAGAZINE SHOULD CONTINUE TO BE PUBLISHED!

IT LOOKS LIKE IT'S UP TO YOU TO CAST THE DECIDING VOTE!

THIS ISN'T WORKING...

WHAT SHOULD I DO? SHOULD I CONTINUE TO LET THE LITERARY MAGAZINE BE PUBLISHED EVEN THOUGH SOME PEOPLE MIGHT BE OFFENDED BY SOME OF THE LANGUAGE IN IT?

STICKS AND STONES CAN BREAK MY BONES, BUT WORDS CAN NEVER HURT ME!

THE DECISION ABOUT THE LITERARY MAGAZINE HAS JUST BEEN TAKEN OUT OF MY HANDS, LES!

PRINCIPAL

MRS. BLACKBURN HAS GONE DIRECTLY TO THE SCHOOL BOARD WITH HER COMPLAINT!

WHAT DO YOU THINK THEY'LL DO?

WESTVIEW HIGH SCHOOL

WELL, WE'RE TALKING ABOUT A SCHOOL BOARD THAT ONCE BANNED 'THE RED BADGE OF COURAGE' BECAUSE THEY THOUGHT IT WAS ABOUT COMMUNISTS!

BATIUK

I'D APPRECIATE IT IF YOU'D JUST SIT TIGHT UNTIL THE SCHOOL BOARD DECIDES WHAT TO DO ABOUT THE LITERARY MAGAZINE, LES... THE LAST THING THE SCHOOL NEEDS AT THIS POINT IS NEGATIVE PUBLICITY!

LES... COULD I TALK WITH YOU?

CINDY SUMMERS!? SURE, I GUESS WE COULD TALK!

IMPORT NOTIC TO A STUDEN

BATIUK

THIS IS CINDY SUMMERS LIVE AT WESTVIEW HIGH SCHOOL WHERE I'M TALKING WITH THE TEACHER AT THE CENTER OF THE LITERARY MAGAZINE CONTROVERSY!

SO YOU'RE A TV REPORTER, CINDY?

YEAH... I TOOK SOME MASS COM COURSES AT COMMUNITY COLLEGE AND CHANNEL SEVEN JUST HIRED ME!

ARE WE GONNA BE ON TELEVISION?

THANKS AGAIN, LES... THIS EXCLUSIVE WILL BE A BIG BEGINNING FOR MY CAREER!

AND THE END OF MINE!

BATIUK

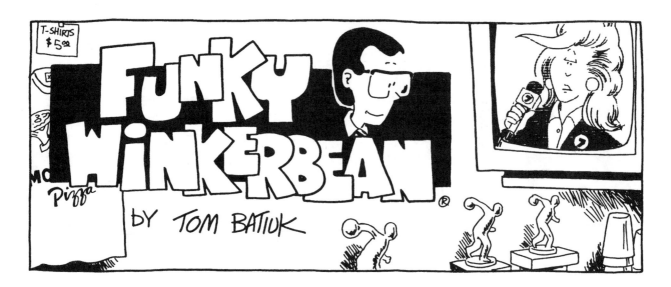

WAY TO GO, PARD... YOU'RE FAMOUS!

YEAH... ME AND O.J. !

SO CINDY SUMMERS IS A TV REPORTER NOW?

YEAH...SHE SNAGGED ME IN THE HALL AND HAD THE CAMERA ROLLING BEFORE I KNEW WHAT HIT ME !

THE PROBLEM IS ... THE SCHOOL DIDN'T WANT ANY PUBLICITY, AND NOW THE LITERARY MAGAZINE CONTROVERSY IS THE HOTTEST ISSUE IN TOWN !

I WISH THERE WAS SOMETHING I COULD DO!

GEE, THANKS, FUNKY...BUT I'M AFRAID THAT THIS IS SOMETHING I'VE GOT TO...

NO... I MEAN SOMETHING LIKE... "AFTER THE SCHOOL BOARD PROTEST, STOP BY MONTONI'S FOR..."

THERE'S A BUNCH OF LETTERS TO THE EDITOR ABOUT YOUR LITERARY MAGAZINE, LES!

MONTONI'S Pizza

YOU REALLY SEEM TO HAVE THE PEOPLE IN THIS TOWN FIRED UP!

OHHH...

UH, TONY ...TRY NOT TO SAY THE WORD 'FIRED' AROUND LES!

SINCE YOU GUYS ARE SO INTERESTED IN DISCUSSING THE LITERARY MAGAZINE CONTROVERSY... LET'S JUST TAKE THIS CLASS PERIOD AND DISCUSS FREEDOM OF EXPRESSION, BECAUSE WHATEVER DECISION IS REACHED, IT'S GOING TO IMPACT YOU THE MOST! YES, SADIE?

IF YOU LOSE YOUR JOB OVER THIS... ARE WE GOING TO GET THAT MEAN SUB?

I DON'T THINK MRS. BLACKBURN IS RIGHT ABOUT THE LITERARY MAGAZINE, MR. MOORE!

YEAH... I DON'T THINK THE NEWSPAPER SHOULD PRINT HER LETTERS ABOUT IT!

ON THE CONTRARY... THAT'S WHAT FREEDOM OF EXPRESSION IS ALL ABOUT... ALLOWING SOMEONE THE RIGHT TO GIVE VOICE TO THEIR IDEAS, NO MATTER HOW MUCH YOU MAY PERSONALLY DISAGREE WITH THEM!

YOU MEAN LIKE WHEN MARBLEHEAD CALLS DARLENE A...

NO, THAT'S SLANDER!

I WOULDN'T SWEAT THE SCHOOL BOARD MEETING OVER THAT LITERARY MAGAZINE THAT YOUR POETRY CLUB PUT OUT, LES!

JUST THINK OF IT AS A PARENT-TEACHER CONFERENCE!

SAY... THAT'S NOT A BAD IDEA, BULL!

THE ONLY DIFFERENCE IS THAT EVERY PARENT IN TOWN IS GOING TO BE THERE!

THERE'S FIVE MORE LETTERS TO THE EDITOR ABOUT YOU AND YOUR LITERARY MAGAZINE IN TODAY'S PAPER!

SWELL...

HOW DID IT COME TO THIS? ALL I DID WAS START A POETRY CLUB... AND NOW I'M SITTING HERE WONDERING IF MY JOB IS GOING TO GO AWAY!

DON'T WORRY... WE CAN ALWAYS USE MORE DELIVERY PEOPLE!

WHAT SORT OF BENEFITS DO YOU HAVE?

When I told Mr. Moore I felt bad because my poem was causing him so much trouble...

he said it wasn't my fault...

and that what was involved here was bigger than both of us!

FUNKY WINKERBEAN by TOM BATIUK

WHY WORRY ABOUT FIGHTING TO SAVE THE WESTVIEW LITERARY MAGAZINE, LES?

AFTER ALL, IT'S JUST A STUDENT MAGAZINE!

THE SCHOOL LITERARY MAGAZINE MAY JUST BE A STUDENT PUBLICATION, FUNKY, BUT IT'S IMPORTANT TO FIGHT THOSE WHO WANT TO SUPPRESS IT... LET ME READ YOU THIS QUOTE BY PASTOR MARTIN NIEMOELLER!

"IN GERMANY THEY CAME FOR THE COMMUNISTS, AND I DIDN'T SPEAK UP BECAUSE I WASN'T A COMMUNIST. THEN THEY CAME FOR THE JEWS, AND I DIDN'T SPEAK UP BECAUSE I WASN'T A JEW.

"THEN THEY CAME FOR THE TRADE UNIONISTS, AND I DIDN'T SPEAK UP BECAUSE I WASN'T A TRADE UNIONIST. THEN THEY CAME FOR THE CATHOLICS, AND I DIDN'T SPEAK UP BECAUSE I WAS A PROTESTANT.

"THEN THEY CAME FOR ME, AND BY THAT TIME NO ONE WAS LEFT TO SPEAK UP."

35

FUNKY WINKERBEAN
BY TOM BATIUK

WHY WORRY ABOUT FIGHTING TO SAVE THE WESTVIEW LITERARY MAGAZINE, LES?

AFTER ALL, IT'S JUST A STUDENT MAGAZINE!

THE SCHOOL LITERARY MAGAZINE MAY JUST BE A STUDENT PUBLICATION, FUNKY, BUT IT'S IMPORTANT TO FIGHT THOSE WHO WANT TO SUPPRESS IT... LET ME READ YOU THIS QUOTE BY PASTOR MARTIN NIEMOELLER!

"IN GERMANY THEY CAME FOR THE COMMUNISTS, AND I DIDN'T SPEAK UP BECAUSE I WASN'T A COMMUNIST. THEN THEY CAME FOR THE JEWS, AND I DIDN'T SPEAK UP BECAUSE I WASN'T A JEW.

"THEN THEY CAME FOR THE TRADE UNIONISTS, AND I DIDN'T SPEAK UP BECAUSE I WASN'T A TRADE UNIONIST. THEN THEY CAME FOR THE CATHOLICS, AND I DIDN'T SPEAK UP BECAUSE I WAS A PROTESTANT.

"THEN THEY CAME FOR ME, AND BY THAT TIME NO ONE WAS LEFT TO SPEAK UP."

BOY... IT SEEMS LIKE THE WHOLE TOWN IS HERE TONIGHT!

SCHOOL BOARD MEETING — TONIGHT 7:30

IS IT WARM IN HERE, FUNKY...

OR IS IT JUST MY SEAT THAT'S HOT?

THE BOARD RECOGNIZES ROBERTA BLACKBURN!

HERE WE GO!

YOU ALL KNOW WHERE I STAND ON THIS ISSUE, SO ALL I HAVE TO SAY IS THAT IF THIS SCHOOL BOARD PERMITS THE PUBLICATION OF TRASH LIKE THIS SO-CALLED LITERARY MAGAZINE...

THEN THE WHOLE LOT OF YOU ARE GOING TO BE DARNED TO HECK FOR ALL ETERNITY!!

I'VE READ THE POEM IN QUESTION IN THE LITERARY MAGAZINE AND I DON'T HAVE ANY PROBLEM WITH IT!

I HAPPEN TO THINK IT'S A BEAUTIFUL POEM THAT HONESTLY EXPLORES THE EMOTIONS OF UNREQUITED LOVE AND THE AWAKENING OF TEENAGE SEXUALITY!

THAT'S EXACTLY THE PROBLEM!

I DON'T THINK THAT TEENAGE SEXUALITY IS SOMETHING THAT OUR TEENAGERS SHOULD BE READING ABOUT!

WELL, KIDDO...

IT LOOKS LIKE WE'VE CLOSED ANOTHER PLACE DOWN!

DID YOU HAVE A GOOD TIME, LISA?

I HAD A WONDERFUL TIME!

THIS PROM WAS EVEN NICER THAN OUR FIRST ONE!

I CAN'T IMAGINE ANYONE WHO WAS HERE TONIGHT WHO DIDN'T ENJOY IT!

FUNKY WINKERBEAN
BY TOM BATIUK

SO WHAT ARE YOU GOING TO DO, LISA?

IT DEPENDS...

IF LES HAS THE SAME FEELINGS FOR ME THAT I DO FOR HIM ... THEN I'LL TURN DOWN THE JOB OFFER OVERSEAS AND STAY HERE!

BUT IF HE DOESN'T SHARE THOSE FEELINGS ... THEN THERE'S NO REASON TO STAY, AND MAYBE GOING TO FRANCE WOULD BE A GOOD WAY TO MAKE A FRESH START!

I NEED SOME SORT OF SIGNAL FROM HIM!

I'VE DECIDED WHAT I'M GOING TO DO!

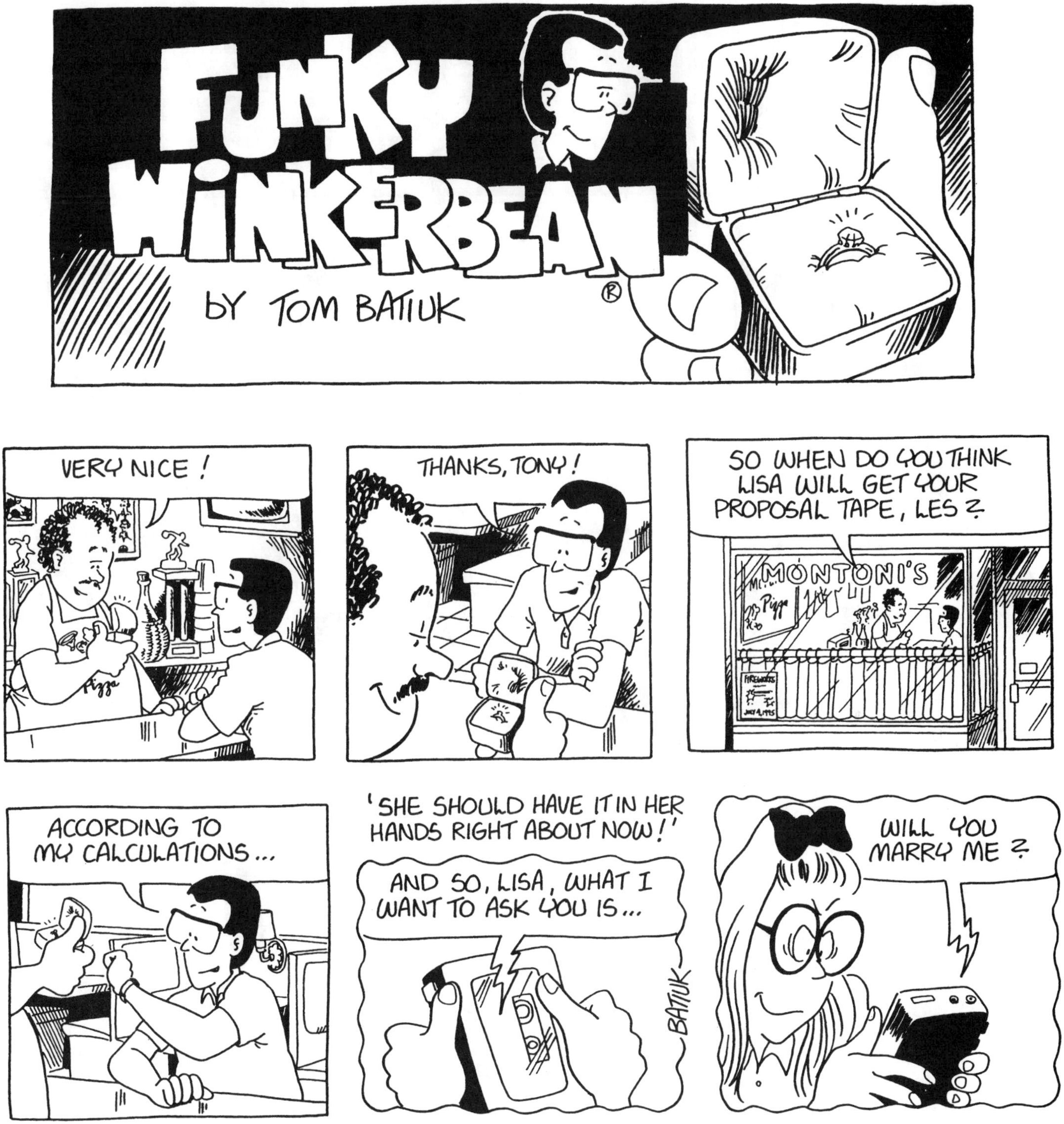
FUNKY WINKERBEAN
BY TOM BATIUK
VERY NICE!
THANKS, TONY!
SO WHEN DO YOU THINK LISA WILL GET YOUR PROPOSAL TAPE, LES?
MONTONI'S
ACCORDING TO MY CALCULATIONS...
'SHE SHOULD HAVE IT IN HER HANDS RIGHT ABOUT NOW!'
AND SO, LISA, WHAT I WANT TO ASK YOU IS...
WILL YOU MARRY ME?
BATIUK

YOU MUST BE PRETTY CONFIDENT THAT LISA WILL SAY 'YES' TO YOUR TAPED PROPOSAL IF YOU'VE ALREADY BOUGHT THE RING, LES!

I AM, TONY... I REALLY FEEL HAPPY AND POSITIVE ABOUT THE FUTURE!

'FOR ONCE IN MY LIFE... I FEEL THAT THINGS ARE FINALLY GOING MY WAY!'

STILL NO WORD FROM LES?

NO...

STILL NO WORD FROM LISA?

NO...

I THOUGHT FOR SURE I WOULD'VE HEARD SOMETHING BY NOW!

I THOUGHT FOR SURE I WOULD'VE HEARD SOMETHING BY NOW!

LOOK, LES, MAYBE THERE'S BEEN SOME KIND OF MIX-UP... MAYBE LISA NEVER GOT THE TAPE YOU SENT!

WHY DON'T YOU GO UPSTAIRS AND GIVE HER A CALL BEFORE YOU GO CRAZY?

MONTONI'S Pizza

48

LOOK, LES ... YOU CAN'T JUST SIT HERE IN THE APARTMENT ALL DAY HOPING THAT THE PHONE IS GOING TO RING!

IF YOU KEEP THIS UP YOU'RE GOING TO MAKE YOURSELF NUTS!

BELIEVE ME...IF LISA WAS GOING TO CALL, YOU WOULD'VE HEARD FROM HER BY NOW!

I SUPPOSE YOU'RE RIGHT...

KENNEDY INTERNATIONAL AIRPORT
GATE

RING! RING!

KENNEDY INTERNATIONAL AIRPORT
GATES 40-5

50

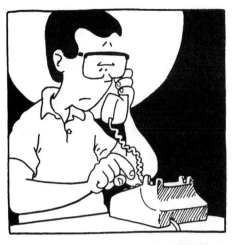

HELLO... OPERATOR? THIS IS 555-1212... WOULD YOU CALL THIS NUMBER BACK AND LET ME KNOW IF IT'S WORKING?

SIR... THIS IS THE FIFTH TIME WE'VE DONE THIS TODAY!

BATIUK

RIINNG!

HELLO!?

BATIUK

NO... I DON'T NEED MY BASEMENT WATERPROOFED...

HERE... I PICKED UP AN ANSWERING MACHINE SO YOU CAN AT LEAST GET OUT OF THE APARTMENT ONCE IN AWHILE!

THANKS, FUNKY... YOU KNOW, YOU'RE REALLY A GOOD FRIEND!

BATIUK

BY THE WAY... MERRY CHRISTMAS FOR NINETEEN NINETY-FIVE AND NINETY-SIX!

GO AHEAD, LISA ... TRY CALLING LES ONE MORE TIME! WHAT HAVE YOU GOT TO LOSE?

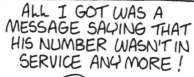

ALL I GOT WAS A MESSAGE SAYING THAT HIS NUMBER WASN'T IN SERVICE ANY MORE!

I'M SORRY...

THERE... THE ANSWERING MACHINE IS HOOKED UP! NOW YOU DON'T HAVE TO WORRY ABOUT MISSING ANY CALLS!

LOOK, I WAS MORE THAN HAPPY TO GET THIS ANSWERING MACHINE FOR THE APARTMENT...

BECAUSE I KNOW YOU DON'T WANT TO MISS ANY POSSIBLE CALLS FROM LISA...

BUT I REALLY THINK OUR MESSAGE SHOULD BE SOMETHING OTHER THAN... 'IF THIS ISN'T LISA, HANG UP AND DON'T CALL BACK!'

BEFORE I BOUGHT THAT ANSWERING MACHINE, LES WAS SPENDING THE WHOLE DAY IN THE APARTMENT SITTING BY THE TELEPHONE...

NOW HE SPENDS THE WHOLE DAY IN THE APARTMENT SITTING BY THE ANSWERING MACHINE!

LES ... YOU JUST CAN'T SIT AROUND MOPING LIKE THIS ALL DAY LONG!

YOU'RE GONNA GO NUTS!

WHAT YOU NEED TO DO IS GET YOUR MIND ON SOMETHING ELSE ... LIKE YOUR WRITING!

WE'LL JUST SIT YOU DOWN ... OPEN UP THIS PUPPY AND...

'ONCE UPON A TIME...'

CLICK!
CLICK!
CLACK!

OKAY ... I'VE GOT YOU STARTED ... NOW YOU TAKE IT FROM THERE!

SO LES IS STILL DOWN IN THE DUMPS, HUH?

YEAH...HE'S TAKING LISA'S LEAVING PRETTY HARD!

I'LL TELL YA... BEING AN ADULT ISN'T ALL THAT IT'S CRACKED UP TO BE!

'I SURE WOULDN'T MIND BEING A CAREFREE KID BACK IN HIGH SCHOOL AGAIN!'

RINNNG!

HELLO?

MR. MOORE, WE'VE NEVER MET, BUT I'M SUSAN SMITH'S MOTHER!

'WE'RE REALLY WORRIED ABOUT HER!'

SUSAN HAS ALWAYS LOOKED UP TO YOU, MR. MOORE, AND WE THOUGHT THAT MAYBE IF YOU COULD TALK WITH HER...

WHAT SEEMS TO BE THE PROBLEM?

WE'RE NOT SURE... ALL WE KNOW IS THAT SHE JUST DOESN'T SEEM TO BE HERSELF!

'FOR ONE THING, SHE ALWAYS USED TO KEEP EVERYTHING IN HER BEDROOM AS NEAT AS A PIN...'

57

FUNKY WINKERBEAN

You are a child of the universe no less than the trees and stars.
Max Erhmann

THANKS FOR COMING BY, MR. MOORE...

AND FOR BRINGING ME HERE THE OTHER DAY!

ACTUALLY, SUSAN, BEING ABLE TO HELP YOU HAS BEEN GOOD FOR ME, TOO... IT ALLOWED ME TO GET MY MIND OFF MY OWN TROUBLES...

AND BY HELPING YOU, I DID THE WORLD A FAVOR, TOO...

BECAUSE THERE'S A LOT OF POETRY IN YOU THAT WON'T BE LOST NOW!

MR. MOORE... **WAIT!** THERE'S SOMETHING I HAVE TO TELL YOU...!!

MR. MOORE ... THERE'S SOMETHING I HAVE TO TELL YOU ...!!

... AND SO, WHEN I SAID I WAS IN LOVE WITH SOMEONE ... WHAT I DIDN'T SAY WAS THAT YOU WERE THAT SOMEONE...

SUSAN ... I ... I DON'T KNOW WHAT TO ...

WAIT ... THERE'S MORE!

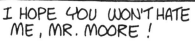

THE DAY YOU PUT YOUR PROPOSAL TAPE IN THE MAIL TO YOUR GIRLFRIEND... I WENT INTO THE OFFICE AND TOOK IT OUT OF THE MAIL TRAY...

SO SHE NEVER GOT THE TAPE!

I'M SORRY...

I HOPE YOU WON'T HATE ME, MR. MOORE!

EVERYONE MAKES MISTAKES, SUSAN...

BUT THE IMPORTANT THING IS THAT YOU'VE JUST MADE AMENDS FOR YOURS!

"E QUINDI USCIMMO A RIVEDER LE STELLE!"

"AND SO WE CAME FORTH, AND ONCE AGAIN BEHELD THE STARS."

WE CAN'T AFFORD THIS... WHAT ARE YOU THINKING!? I NEVER USED TO HAVE THESE KINDS OF EXPENSES!

YOU NEVER USED TO HAVE THESE KINDS OF PROFITS!

SO WHAT'S YOUR POINT?

THIS MONTH'S EXPENSES FOR ADVERTISING ARE NEARLY DOUBLE FROM THE MONTH BEFORE!

WHAT COULD POSSIBLY BE WORTH THAT KIND OF MONEY!?

MONTONI'S Pizza

OH...

BY THE WAY, MICKEY...THANKS FOR SUGGESTING THAT I GET THAT FORMER HIGH SCHOOL ART TEACHER TO PAINT THAT SIGN ON THE SIDE OF THE BUILDING!

I THINK TONY REALLY LIKES IT!

WHERE'S TONY?

HE'S ORDERING A PIZZA!

ORDERING A PIZZA?

MORE CHEESE AND MORE PEPPERONIS IN THE MIDDLE!

WELL, TONY...WHAT DO YOU THINK?

I THINK WE SHOULD CONTACT THE CITY ABOUT GETTING A STREETLIGHT HERE ON THE CORNER SO PEOPLE CAN SEE IT BETTER AT NIGHT!

HE LIKES IT!

WELL, I'M GLAD YOU LIKED THE SIGN, TONY...

AND I PROMISE THERE WILL BE NO MORE OUT-OF-THE-ORDINARY EXPENSES LIKE THAT!

ACTUALLY, THERE WILL BE...

I'VE HIRED THE ARTIST TO PAINT SOME SCENES OF ITALY ON THE WALL IN THE OLD PART OF THE RESTAURANT!

WE CAN'T AFFORD THAT! WHAT ARE YOU THINKING!?

I'VE EMPTIED MY BANK ACCOUNT AND PICKED UP MY PASSPORT AND AIRLINE TICKETS!

LET'S SEE YOUR PASSPORT PHOTO!

YIKES! HAVE YOU EVER THOUGHT ABOUT DRIVING A CAB IN NEW YORK CITY!?

I DON'T THINK I'D LET SOMEONE WHO LOOKED LIKE THAT ON A PLANE!

I TALKED WITH LISA'S PARENTS... LISA DOESN'T HAVE A PHONE IN HER APARTMENT YET... BUT I'VE GOT THE ADDRESS FOR WHERE SHE'S STAYING!

WITH ANY LUCK AT ALL I'LL BE SEEING HER IN A COUPLE OF DAYS!

LOOK, LISA... SCHOOL WON'T BE STARTING FOR A FEW WEEKS YET! MAYBE IT WOULD HELP YOU GET OVER YOUR BOYFRIEND IF WE JUST TOOK OFF AND DID SOME TRAVELING!

TRUST ME, LISA... A COUPLE OF DAYS ON THE BEACH...

AND YOU'LL FORGET ALL ABOUT THAT GUY BACK HOME!

I'M GOING TO POP OVER AND GET SOMETHING TO DRINK! WANT ANYTHING?

NO THANKS, LISA!

CAPPELLA SISTINA

I'VE NEVER SEEN ANYTHING SO BEAUTIFUL!

THIS IS HOPELESS!

SEARCHING FOR LISA LIKE THIS IS LIKE LOOKING FOR A NEEDLE IN A HAYSTACK! THERE'S NO WAY I CAN HOPE TO FIND HER!

✳ SIGH ✳ I SUPPOSE THAT AS LONG AS I'M HERE, I SHOULDN'T PASS UP AN OPPORTUNITY TO SEE THE SISTINE CHAPEL!

FUNKY SAYS HE FOUND THIS SITTING ON THE CURB WITH SOMEONE'S TRASH!

I THINK IT'LL GIVE THE PLACE AN ECLECTIC LOOK!

I GUESS THAT WOULD MAKE YOU AN ECKLEPTOMANIAC!

THIS LAMP IS SIGNED C.L. TIFFANY, FUNKY... YOU DON'T SUPPOSE THIS COULD BE A GENUINE TIFFANY LAMP, DO YOU?

GET REAL... WHY WOULD SOMEBODY THROW OUT SOMETHING THAT WAS ACTUALLY WORTH ANYTHING?

APPARENTLY I NEVER TOLD YOU THE STORY ABOUT MY MOTHER AND MY COMIC BOOK COLLECTION!

GET THAT ONE!

NO WAY! THE TEENAGE MUTANT NINJA TURTLES AREN'T AS GOOD AS THE X-MEN!

AND TODAY THAT FIRST ISSUE WOULD BE WORTH...?

FOUR FIGURES, EASY!

I STILL SAY THE X-MEN COULD TAKE THE TURTLES ANY DAY OF THE WEEK!

I CAN'T BELIEVE THIS IS REALLY HAPPENING!

SO HOW DO YOU FEEL?

LIKE THROWING UP!

SO THAT'S WHY YOU NEVER GOT MY PROPOSAL TAPE, AND WHY I CAME HERE TO FIND YOU!

THEN THAT REALLY WAS YOU I SAW EVERYWHERE!

JUST MY LUCK I FINALLY HAVE A STORY ABOUT 'HOW I SPENT MY SUMMER' AND I'M NO LONGER IN SCHOOL!

TRUE...BUT YOU ARE A WRITER!

ARE YOU KIDDING?

TRUE... WHO'D BE DUMB ENOUGH TO EXPECT PEOPLE TO BELIEVE A STORY LIKE THAT?

78

FUNKY WINKERBEAN
BY TOM BATIUK

AND SO THAT'S THE WHOLE STORY!

AMAZING!

WELL, CONGRATULATIONS ON YOUR ENGAGEMENT, SIR!

THANKS!

MONTONI'S PIZZA

I WAS UNDER THE IMPRESSION THAT TONY WANTED THIS MURAL TO BE SCENES OF ITALY!

HE DID!

THEN HOW DO YOU EXPLAIN THE PAGODAS AND THE LLAMAS?

I THINK IT WAS A CASE OF AN ARTIST WITH NINE FEET OF MURAL...

HAVING TO COVER TWELVE FEET OF WALL!

80

RIINNG!

SUSAN...

WELCOME BACK!

LISA'S CLASSES IN FRANCE ARE FINALLY OVER, AND TO SAVE MONEY SHE'S GOING TO BE FLYING STANDBY THE WHOLE TRIP HOME...

SO SHE'LL BE GETTING BACK EITHER TODAY OR TOMORROW... I'M SO ANXIOUS I CAN BARELY CONCENTRATE ON ANYTHING!

I CAN TELL...

YOU JUST COPIED YOUR TIE ALONG WITH ALL OF YOUR TEST COPIES!

DOOP!

HI, FUNKY... I CAME BY TO PICK UP MICKEY!

SHE'S INSIDE, LINDA!

WHAT'S LES DOING?

HE'S EXPECTING LISA ANYTIME NOW... SO HE'S AVERAGING GRADES AT THE BAR SO HE'LL SEE HER AS SOON AS SHE GETS HERE!

WHAT DO YOU SAY WE HAVE A LITTLE FUN?

SURPRISE!

LISA!!?

OH... IT'S YOU!

YOU SURE KNOW HOW TO MAKE A LADY FEEL WELCOME!

AT THIS POINT, GENTLE READERS, IT'S PERHAPS BEST THAT WE AVERT OUR EYES FROM THE SCENE THAT FOLLOWS... EXCEPT TO SAY THAT, AFTER A RATHER LENGTHY DISCUSSION, MATTERS WERE FINALLY SETTLED TO EVERYONE'S SATISFACTION!

HAVING OUR WEDDING RECEPTION HERE IS THE PERFECT WEDDING GIFT, TONY...

AND WITH OUR FINANCES AS TIGHT AS THEY ARE ... IT REALLY HELPS US OUT!

WHICH REMINDS ME... THERE ARE STILL A COUPLE OF OTHER PROBLEMS THAT I'VE GOT TO DEAL WITH!

IF WE'RE GOING TO BE ABLE TO AFFORD TO GET MARRIED ... I'M GOING TO HAVE TO GET A JOB IN PRETTY SHORT ORDER!

ACTUALLY, I CAN HELP THERE, TOO !

WORK HERE!? TONY, I CAN'T ACCEPT A JOB FROM YOU!

WHY NOT? FUNKY HAS THIS PLACE JUMPING SO MUCH THAT I NEED ALL THE GOOD WAITRESSES I CAN FIND!

TONY, HOW CAN WE EVER REPAY YOU?

BY BEING HERE PROMPTLY AT FOUR O'CLOCK TOMORROW TO START WORK!

NOW THAT I'VE GOT A JOB ... ALL I NEED IS A PLACE TO STAY!

WELL ... SINCE TONY IS HANDING OUT WEDDING GIFTS ...

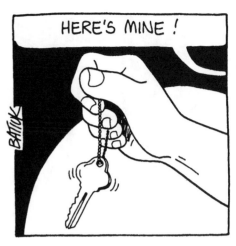

HERE'S MINE!

LOOK, I WANT YOU GUYS TO HAVE THE APARTMENT UPSTAIRS!

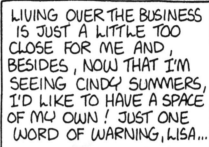

LIVING OVER THE BUSINESS IS JUST A LITTLE TOO CLOSE FOR ME AND, BESIDES, NOW THAT I'M SEEING CINDY SUMMERS, I'D LIKE TO HAVE A SPACE OF MY OWN! JUST ONE WORD OF WARNING, LISA...

HE SNORES LIKE A CHAIN SAW!

I DO NOT!

I DON'T WANT TO MAKE YOU MOVE OUT OF THE APARTMENT, FUNKY!

LISTEN TO HER...

LISA'S RIGHT, FUNKY ... I DON'T KNOW...

GOOD POINT!

SORRY, BUT I WON'T TAKE 'KNOW' FOR AN ANSWER!

MAYBE WE SHOULD ALL HAVE SOME PIZZA AND TALK ABOUT THIS ...

TRUST ME... YOU'RE MAKING THE RIGHT DECISION, LISA...

AND YOU'RE GOING TO LOVE THE COMMUTE TO WORK!

WELL, I THINK I FINALLY CONVINCED LES AND LISA TO ACCEPT THE APARTMENT AS MY WEDDING GIFT TO THEM...

NOW I GUESS I HAVE TO CONVINCE YOU, HUH?

I DON'T KNOW WHAT CAME OVER ME...

I MEAN, I KNOW IT'S THE NINETIES AND EVERYTHING... AND THAT IT'S NO BIG DEAL FOR PEOPLE TO LIVE TOGETHER BEFORE THEY GET MARRIED ANYMORE...

BUT FOR A SECOND THERE I SUDDENLY BECAME MY FATHER!

HAPPY FATHER'S DAY, TONY!

AND THE PROBLEM ISN'T JUST LIMITED TO THE INTERNET...

WE'RE BEING BOMBARDED WITH THIS FILTH FROM ALL SIDES, PEOPLE!

WHY DO YOU LISTEN TO THAT GUY, TONY?

HAVE YOU TAKEN A LOOK AT THE SUNDAY COMICS LATELY?

HE'S FUNNY...AND BESIDES, HE'S ONLY EXERCISING HIS FIRST AMENDMENT RIGHTS!

WHAT IN HEAVEN'S NAME IS GOING ON THERE?

WHY IS IT THAT WHENEVER HE EXERCISES HIS FREE SPEECH...

TEEN PREGNANCY, GUNS IN SCHOOLS, TEEN SUICIDE...

I FEEL LIKE I'M ABOUT TO LOSE SOME OF MINE?

WHEN DID THIS GARBAGE SUDDENLY BECOME FODDER FOR THE FUNNIES?

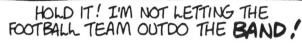

I SAW THE APPEAL FOR BLOOD ON TV AND I BROUGHT THE TEAM OVER TO DONATE!

HOLD IT! I'M NOT LETTING THE FOOTBALL TEAM OUTDO THE **BAND**!

TAKE AN EXTRA PINT FROM HIM... HE WON'T MISS IT!

I'M GOING TO STAY HERE AT THE HOSPITAL WITH LES, TONY... LISA JUST CAME OUT OF THE OPERATING ROOM AND THE DOCTORS SAID IT WAS GOING TO BE TOUCH-AND-GO FOR A WHILE!

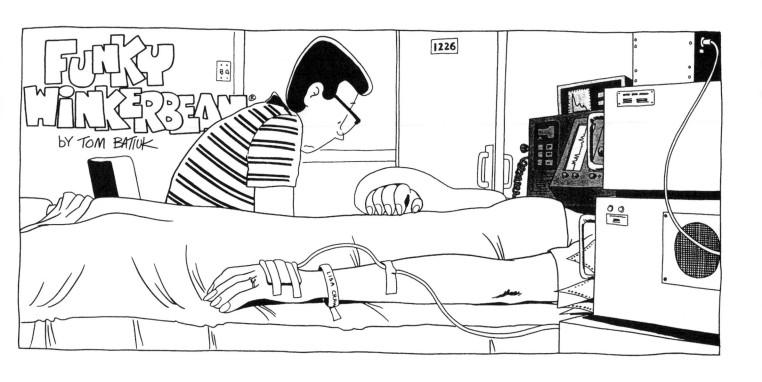

I'LL NEVER FORGET HOW NERVOUS I WAS THE FIRST TIME I ASKED LISA OUT...

UH, SAY, IF YOU DON'T HAVE A DATE FOR THE PROM, WOULD YOU, UH... LIKE TO GO WITH ME?

SURE!

THAT'S OKAY, I UNDERSTAND... MAYBE SOME OTHER TIME...

NO! WAIT!!

WHEN I TOOK LISA TO THE PROM IN HIGH SCHOOL, THE WORLD WAS COOL AND GOOD AND OUR FATE RESTED IN OUR OWN HANDS...

AND WHEN YOU GET OUT OF COLLEGE, WHAT DO YOU WANT TO DO?

BECOME A WRITER! WHAT DO YOU THINK ABOUT THAT?

I THINK YOU'D BETTER RETURN YOUR SEATBACK TO THE UPRIGHT POSITION AND PREPARE TO LAND!

I'LL ALWAYS REMEMBER HOW YOU STOOD BY LISA WHEN SHE HAD THAT OTHER GUY'S BABY...

I ALWAYS THOUGHT THAT THE DAY I FOUND OUT I WAS GOING TO HAVE A BABY WOULD BE ONE OF THE HAPPIEST OF MY LIFE...

AND INSTEAD, WHEN I FOUND OUT... I CRIED!

100

HOW IS SHE?

SHE STILL HASN'T REGAINED CONSCIOUSNESS!

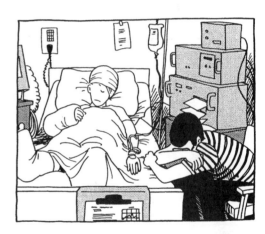

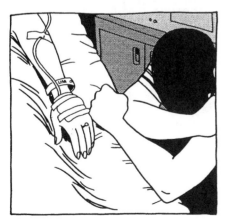

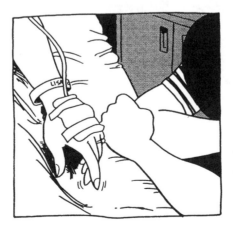

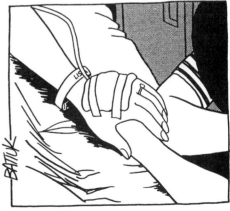

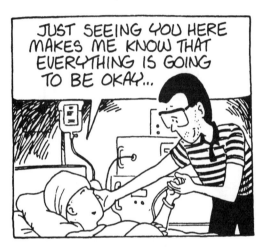

103

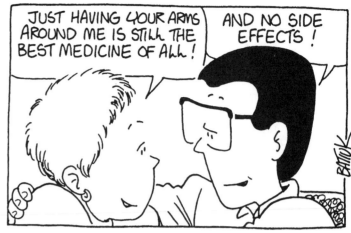

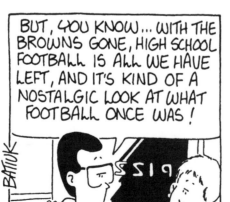

BIG WALNUT TECH JUST WANTED TO RUN THE SCORE UP ON US...

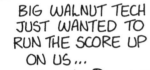

WE DIDN'T HAVE TO PLAY THE FOURTH QUARTER!

I GUESS IT JUST WASN'T IN THE CARDS...

TONIGHT WAS MY LAST CHANCE EVER TO BEAT BIG WALNUT TECH... AND I BLEW IT!

I'M GOING TO RETIRE WITHOUT EVER ONCE KNOWING WHAT IT FEELS LIKE TO BE CARRIED OFF THE FIELD ON THE SHOULDERS OF MY PLAYERS...

SO HAVE YOU TWO DECIDED ON A NEW WEDDING DATE YET?

WE'RE GOING TO WAIT UNTIL LISA FEELS UP TO IT, AND THEN WE'LL PICK ONE!

ACTUALLY, I ALREADY HAVE...

REALLY!?

YOU'RE NOT JOKING? YOU REALLY WANT TO GET MARRIED ON HALLOWEEN?

SURE! IT'S ALWAYS BEEN MY FAVORITE TIME OF THE YEAR...

AND I FIGURE THIS WAY YOU'LL ALWAYS BE ABLE TO REMEMBER OUR ANNIVERSARY!

ANOTHER WEDDING INVITATION ALL SET TO GO!

THIS IDEA OF SEALING THINGS WITH A KISS COULD REALLY CATCH ON!

WHAT'S ALL THIS ABOUT?

INVITATIONS TO OUR WEDDING AND RECEPTION AT MONTONI'S!

YOU'RE GETTING MARRIED ON OCTOBER 31!?

BOY, YOU SURE KNOW HOW TO MAKE HALLOWEEN SCARY!!

SO THEN BULL SAID...'BOY, YOU SURE KNOW HOW TO MAKE HALLOWEEN SCARY!'

DO YOU THINK THAT WHAT WE'RE DOING IS SCARY?

IT ONLY SCARES ME WHEN I THINK ABOUT WHAT LIFE WOULD'VE BEEN LIKE IF YOU HADN'T COME ALONG!

LET'S SEE...THE INVITATIONS HAVE AHL BEEN SENT... I MADE ARRANGEMENTS WITH REVEREND WILSON...THE FOOD HAS AHL BEEN TAKEN CARE OF... I PICKED UP THE STUFF WE'LL NEED FOR DECORATIONS...

AND YOU GOT THE MARRIAGE CERTIFICATE... SO IT LOOKS LIKE WE'RE AHL SET!

THERE'S A **TEN-DAY** WAITING PERIOD TO GET A MARRIAGE LICENSE!?

TEN WORKING DAYS!

BUT I'M GETTING MARRIED ON **OCTOBER THIRTY-FIRST**!!

NO YOU'RE NOT!

AND JUDGE SMITH, THE PROBATE JUDGE, WOULD HAVE TO WAIVE THE WAITING PERIOD FOR THE MARRIAGE LICENSE... WHICH THEY NEVER DO SIMPLY BECAUSE YOU FORGOT ABOUT GETTING IT!

THE SAME THING HAPPENED WHEN ANN AND I GOT MARRIED... IN FACT, A STUDENT WHO WAS A COMPUTER HACKER ACTUALLY BROKE INTO THE COURTHOUSE RECORDS AND CHANGED THEM FOR US!

WHERE IS HE NOW?

DON'T KNOW... WE HELD HIM BACK AS LONG AS WE COULD SO HE COULD WORK ON OUR COMPUTERS... BUT WE FINALLY HAD TO GRADUATE HIM!

LISA HAS MADE ALL THE ARRANGEMENTS... PEOPLE ALL COMING IN FROM OUT OF TOWN...

AND NOW WE'RE GOING TO HAVE TO GET IN TOUCH WITH EVERYONE AND CANCEL EVERYTHING!

I WOULDN'T...

THEY'LL PROBABLY WANT TO STAY FOR YOUR FUNERAL!

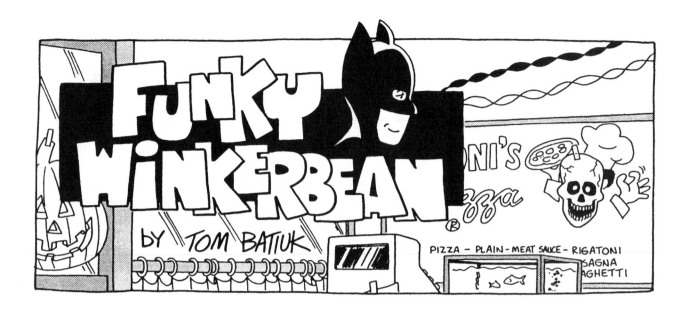

ARE YOU NERVOUS, LES?

DRESSED LIKE THIS!?

SO WHAT DO YOU THINK?

NOT BAD... BUT ISN'T IT BAD LUCK FOR THE GROOM TO SEE THE BRIDE BEFORE THE WEDDING?

LISTEN, WITH WHAT I'VE BEEN THROUGH THE PAST FEW MONTHS...

I'M JUST HAPPY TO BE SEEN!

DOESN'T MATTER. I CAN'T SEE A THING WITHOUT MY GLASSES ANYWAY!

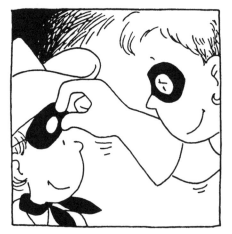

114

SO WHERE ARE YOU GUYS OFF TO ?

WHY, GOTHAM CITY, OF COURSE!

I JUST NEGLECTED TO SAY THAT WE WOULDN'T BE LEAVING UNTIL SPRING BREAK!

FUNKY...THIS IS TONY! COME ON DOWN FOR A SECOND...I WANT TO SHOW YOU SOMETHING!

OH NO YOU DON'T! YOU'RE NOT ALLOWED IN THE RESTAURANT!

BUT I'LL BRING BACK SOME ANCHOVIES FOR YOU!

AN AQUARIUM!?

YEAH...I'VE ALWAYS WANTED ONE!

THEY'RE REALLY FUN TO WATCH!

OH, I ALMOST FORGOT...I WANT TO TAKE SOME ANCHOVIES BACK FOR 'ANCHOVY'!

HE HATES BEING COOPED UP IN THE APARTMENT...

PLOP!

BUT AT LEAST I KNOW HE'S SAFE!

ULTIMATELY, THE ACT OF CREATION ...

IS A VERY PRIVATE THING.

WE CANNOT EXPERIENCE THE SWEETNESS OF THE ARTIST'S VISIONS...

OR THE TERROR OF HIS NIGHTMARES.

WE CAN ONLY KNOW WHAT THE ARTIST CHOOSES TO PRESENT TO US...

AND SIMPLY WONDER ABOUT THE MAN !

120

I'VE ALSO SCHEDULED AN APPOINTMENT FOR YOU WITH A SPORTS PSYCHOLOGIST, A HYPNOTIST, A BALLET INSTRUCTOR AND A SPORTS NUTRITIONIST!

DO YOU REALLY THINK IF I DO ALL THAT STUFF THAT I'LL BE ABLE TO MAKE THAT SHOT FROM HALF-COURT?

NO... BUT IT SHOULD BRING THE ODDS AGAINST YOU DOWN FROM THE HIGH MILLIONS!

AND ONCE I'D CLIMBED THE ROPE IN GYM CLASS, I'D BECOME PARALYZED WITH FEAR AND UNABLE TO CLIMB BACK DOWN!

IF FACT, ONE TIME I WAS STUCK UP THERE THE WHOLE WEEKEND DURING THE HOMECOMING DANCE!

SINCE WE ONLY HAVE A WEEK ... PERHAPS I SHOULD SEE YOU THREE TIMES A DAY!

WHENEVER WE'D CHOOSE UP SIDES TO PLAY TOUCH FOOTBALL ... THE KIDS WOULD PLAY WITH UNEVEN SIDES RATHER THAN PICK ME...

LOSER!

123

LES SEES A SPORTS PSYCHOLOGIST TO HELP HIM PREPARE FOR HIS TEN-THOUSAND-DOLLAR HALF-COURT SHOT...

AND WHENEVER ANYONE IN GYM CLASS MENTIONED THE WORD TUMBLING...

I'D IMMEDIATELY BREAK OUT IN HIVES!

LET ME ASK YOU THIS... WERE THERE ANY SPORTS OR GAMES THAT YOU WERE GOOD AT?

DR. CLUTCH SHOTZ
SPORTS PSYCHOLOGIST

WELL, AT ONE POINT WHEN I WAS A CHILD, I'D THOUGHT I WAS PRETTY GOOD AT HIDE-AND-SEEK!

I ONCE HID FOR TWELVE HOURS WITHOUT ANYONE EVER FINDING ME...

BUT THEN I FOUND OUT THAT NO ONE HAD BEEN LOOKING FOR ME!

COULD BE A BOOK DEAL HERE!

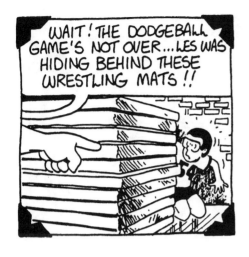

WE DIRECT YOUR ATTENTION TO CENTER COURT WHERE LES MOORE IS ABOUT TO ATTEMPT A SHOT FROM HALF-COURT FOR TEN THOUSAND DOLLARS !!

GOOD LUCK, FELLA !

OKAY, I JUST HAVE TO REMEMBER WHAT BULL SAID ABOUT LETTING MUSCLE MEMORY TAKE OVER...

AND THEN DO THE VISUALIZATION TECHNIQUES THAT THE SPORTS PSYCHOLOGIST SHOWED ME... AND REMEMBER THE RELAXATION TRIGGER WORD THE HYPNOTIST GAVE ME...

OH... AND I'VE GOT TO RUB THE LUCKY QUARTER THAT LISA GAVE ME...

HONK !

SORRY, PAL... HALFTIME'S OVER !

THAT'S TOO BAD, FOLKS... IT LOOKS LIKE THE OLD NERVES KIND OF GOT TO HIM !

SORRY... THEY'RE READY TO START THE SECOND HALF !

WHAT !?

BUT I WAS JUST ABOUT TO TAKE MY SHOT !

HERE... YOU CAN HAVE THIS !

126

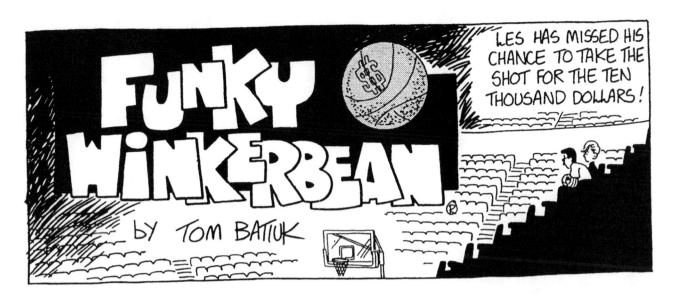